Jesus and His Abba

Jesus and His Abba

A Little Christology

Leonardo Boff

ORBIS BOOKS
Maryknoll, New York 10545

The publishing arm of the Maryknoll Fathers and Brothers, Orbis seeks to explore the global dimensions of Christian faith and mission, to invite dialogue with diverse cultures and religious traditions, and to serve the cause of reconciliation and peace. The books published reflect the views of their authors and do not represent the official position of the Maryknoll Society. To learn more about Maryknoll and Orbis Books, please visit our website at www.orbisbooks.com.

Library of Congress Cataloging-in-Publication Data

Names: Boff, Leonardo, author.

Title: Jesus and his Abba : a little Christology / Leonardo Boff.

Other titles: A amorosidade do Deus-Abba e Jesu de Nazarâe. English.

Description: Maryknoll, NY : Orbis Books, [2024] | "Original title: A amorosidade do Deus-Abbá e Jesus de Nazaré © Leonardo Boff, Petrópolis, Brasil"—Title page verso. | Includes bibliographical references.

Identifiers: LCCN 2024020190 (print) | LCCN 2024020191 (ebook) | ISBN 9781626985780 (trade paperback) | ISBN 9798888660331 (epub)

Subjects: LCSH: Jesus Christ—Person and offices.

Classification: LCC BT203 .B6413 2024 (print) | LCC BT203 (ebook) | DDC 232—dc23/eng/20240618

LC record available at https://lccn.loc.gov/2024020190

LC ebook record available at https://lccn.loc.gov/2024020191

Contents

Introduction

Can we describe in a few words the mystery surrounding the historical figure of Jesus of Nazareth? The Christian faith professes that he is the incarnate Son of God, who shares our human nature and, at the same time, possesses the divine nature of God. How can we combine these two realities? For more than two thousand years, theological reflection has endeavored to articulate them. Despite the many formulas that have been developed, mystery remains mystery, a permanent challenge for Christian thought.

Our text does not pretend to address all these questions. To a large extent, I have already done so in the more than eight hundred pages I have written about Jesus Christ over more than fifty years of theological work.

The question that challenges us is this: at what point in the life of the historical Jesus did this reality of being the beloved Son of God-Abba, slowly taking shape in his consciousness, achieve its full clarity? Whoever calls God Father (using the intimate form of Abba as Dear Daddy) can only feel that he is his Son.

But at what point did this mysterious and intimate feeling become fully conscious in his own life, to the point of producing in him a true inner revolution, a change of life, inaugurating a new language, introducing a new practice, and acting as one who takes the place of God?

1

Relevance of the Resurrection
to Christology

What sustains the Christian faith throughout history and up to the present day is
faith in the resurrection. It is not a question of the
resuscitation of a corpse, as in the case of Lazarus
(Jn 11:43), but of the irruption of the *novissimus
Adam* (1 Cor 15:45): the new human being who
has realized all his potentialities, so that death no
longer has any dominion over him. He has assumed the characteristics of God himself.

Through the resurrection, the Jesus *kata
sarka*, according to the flesh, limited in space

and time in Palestine, became the Christ *kata pneuma*, the Christ according to the Spirit—that is, according to the divine nature. Thus, he becomes the cosmic Christ who fills all the spaces of the human and of the universe. This is clearly expressed in Agraphon 77 of the Coptic Gospel of St. Thomas, where his cosmic presence is revealed: "I am the light that is above all things. I am the universe; the universe came out of me and the universe came back to me. Break the wood and I am in it, lift the stone and I am under it, for I will be with you all the days until the end of time."

The event of the resurrection is, therefore, the starting point of all Jesuology and Christology. Jesus, by his message and his action, by his magnetism and his charisma, provoked the admiration and also the faith of the apostles and the disciples (particularly the women disciples) who followed him. Unlike the male apostles, the female disciples never betrayed him, and they accompanied him to Calvary. Undoubtedly, he was someone who had a special power to heal the sick and to perform exorcisms to free people from serious mental illnesses, considered according to the categories of his time as diabolical possessions.

However, if the resurrection had not taken place, all this would have been forgotten. Jesus would have been one of the many prophets who tried to transform the world and were rejected and killed. Instead, with the resurrection, everything changed. Resurrection is the victory over the kind of death we know and the beginning of another kind of life in which death no longer has a place, a life in fullness. Resurrection is, then, the celebration of a living presence and not the memory of a dead past.

This is the founding fact of Christianity. The resurrection appears as a revolution within evolution. It is not only the resurrection of Jesus, for, according to St. Paul and the entire biblical tradition, it is the resurrection of his entire community. He is the first among many brothers and sisters (cf. Rom 8:29); we participate in it. We do not live in order to die; we die in order to rise.

However, in its Greco-Roman inculturation, the resurrection of Jesus was read apologetically, as the greatest miracle and a kind of rejoinder against his unjust condemnation. The resurrection of the human being was relegated to the end of the world, while in death, as eminent ecumenical theologians maintain, the resurrection occurs when the world and time end for the person. What comes next? Eternity, with the resurrection as an expression of the full realization of all the potentialities hidden in each person.

In the history of Christianity, incarnated in Greco-Latin culture, the resurrection was replaced by the Greek doctrine of the immortality of the soul. As a result, Christianity, once a movement of hope and anticipation of a good end for humanity and for all creation, became an institution, a religion, alongside all the others, with everything that belongs to religion: doctrines, canons, rites, ethical norms, and traditions. But it lost its uniqueness and that utopian impulse, present in faith in the resurrection, capable of energizing and transforming human destiny.

Despite this error, the resurrection has been kept alive in celebrations and liturgies, and especially through the sacrament of the Eucharist, in which the sacramental and real presence of the living and risen Christ among us is reaffirmed.

This event of the resurrection appears as the catalyst of any Christology that presents itself as Christian. Without faith in the resurrection, there would not have been the emergence of the Christian communities, nor would the way of Jesus have been followed, nor would the four Gospels and all the other New Testament texts exist. What challenged the apostles was precisely how to interpret the death on the cross, considered a scandal and a divine curse, and the resurrection as an amazing event after the crucifixion. They searched for scriptural texts and filled the Gospels with biblical quotations to find a meaning for all these events.

2

Flesh (Jesuology) Precedes Spirit (Christology)

Assuming this horizon, Christology can start from the historical Jesus to arrive at the Christ of faith. In this case the flesh precedes the spirit. The concrete, vulnerable, and limited historicity, with its lights and shadows (flesh), sustains the spirit, the salvific and divine dimension of Jesus, the Christ. Jesuology is at the basis of Christology. The latter fades into an imaginative idyll without the concreteness of the former.

Therefore, it is important to start from the historical Jesus. But we must think of history as we understand it today, within a new vision of the universe, of life, and of humanity.

Jesus was potentially present in that tiny dot full of matter, energy, and information that later exploded (the Big Bang). He was also potentially present in the interior of the great red stars, at the heart of which were forged all the physical and chemical elements that compose the entire universe. When they exploded, they dispersed those elements in all directions and formed the galaxies, the stars, the planets like Earth, and each one of us, as well as the humanity of the historical Jesus. Thus, the iron that coursed through his veins, the phosphorus and calcium that strengthened his bones and nerves, the nitrogen and hydrogen that ensured his growth, the 65 percent oxygen and 18 percent carbon without which life would neither arise nor flourish, were present in Jesus.

His origin, therefore, is as old as the universe. His *roots* are in our Milky Way, his *cradle* in the solar system, his *home* on the planet

Earth and his specific *place* in Palestine, more specifically in Nazareth.

He is an Aramean, a member of the Semitic people, whose ancient origins are located in Mesopotamia, southeast of present-day Turkey, northeast of Syria, and north of Iraq. He was not, therefore, a white, blue-eyed, blond-haired European, as depicted in the dominant iconography, nor is he a Greek or a Roman; rather, he is an inhabitant of the Near East, an Aramaic Semite with almost brown skin. He lived in a marginal province of the Roman Empire, Palestine and Galilee, under the *Pax Romana* of the Caesars.

If we start from the historical Jesus, we must take seriously his human nature, formed over billions of years of cosmic and earthly history. But he is also embedded in our concrete, human, Semitic history, with the weight that history entails: complexity, scope, limitation, finitude, crisis, and mortality.

The creed's affirmation that he is consubstantial with us, in our full humanity, implies recognizing that Jesus went through all the stages in the constitution of his identity. First, until the age of two, he is most closely attached to his mother, Mary, who, like the nurturing mother figure, gives him a sense of warmth and welcome. At a later stage the relationship shifts to the father figure, Joseph, in whom he finds the hero, strength, and security. The father's task is to set boundaries and teach respect for all people and reverence for God. The father is also the transitional link to relationships with other people beyond the family—grandparents, relatives—to friends and to men and women in general. He finds his place in society and defines his profession.

Each phase implies a certain crisis of passage. This should be understood as part of the normality of the individuation process. It is by overcoming crises that the person matures and defines his or her life trajectory. It is the crisis of youth, the crisis of maturity, the crisis of choosing a profession. The historical Jesus went through all this; otherwise, he would not be human like us and the incarnation would not be fully human.

It should be emphasized that Jesus, as a historical protagonist, has both an *objective* side and a *subjective* side. He is in the world together with others (objective) and simultaneously feels, reacts, and thinks through his experiences with his own subjectivity (subjective). How did Jesus of Nazareth live his concrete factual reality, objectively and subjectively?

Most of the Christological production, immense and proper to each generation, stems from the dogma of the incarnation of the Son of the Father in the power of the Spirit. Thus it treats of the divine character of Christ or of the historical man, Jesus of Nazareth, of his deeds, of his message, of the hope he raised, and also of the conflicts he provoked, and finally of his condemnation to death on the cross, followed by his resurrection.

Today, ecumenical theology, based on exegetical, historical, and even archaeological studies, especially the theology of liberation, starts from the historical Jesus, from his following, from the centrality of his life, from his practice, clearly linked to the poorest and most suffering and, therefore, liberating. His followers may eventually suffer the same fate: persecution, defamation, and even violent death, as we have seen in the history of Christianity, especially in Latin America, and in other places at risk.

Because of the relevance of the historical Jesus, a French theologian, Jean Onimus, in his 1999 book, *Jésus en direct,* correctly points out:

> The Incarnate Word no longer has an impact on our spirits, but the voice that points out the care of children, that brings happiness to the humble and that places love above all values, will always be heard by all men and in all times. . . . To locate Jesus in the foreground, to see him live, to listen, while it is still possible, to the

tone of his words, his anger, his impatience, but also his moments of affection and pity, but a totally human being who comes to reveal to us, precisely because he is human, what is completely other in the deepest part of us, what is, perhaps, in reality divine.

Now, when we speak of the incarnation, we think precisely of these human qualities of Jesus, although the word *incarnation*, due to its use, has lost the completeness described above.

The great Portuguese poet Fernando Pessoa says the same in his poetic language: "He is the God that was missing. He is the human who is natural. He is the divine who smiles and plays . . . so human that he is divine."

In a similar way to this theologian and this poet, excellent studies have been published considering the concrete world in which the historical Jesus lived as a carpenter-craftsman and Mediterranean peasant.

The context is the occupation of Israel by
the Imperial Roman forces, the various religious and political tendencies internal to the
Judaism of his time, and the conflict that Jesus
himself provoked: by his message of hope, by
his liberating practice, and by the authority
and sovereignty with which he acted as one
who acted in the name of God. He announced
the Father's plan: the kingdom of God, which
is in our midst.

The sources are mainly the four Gospels
(and let us add the apocryphal Gospel of
Thomas, the Didache, and the Q Source,
the base text for the Gospels of Matthew
and Luke, and Codex D) and other New
Testament texts, especially those written by
St. Paul, a great witness of the resurrection,
although he did not know the historical
Jesus. The Gospels began to be written between 35 and 45 years after the execution of
Jesus on the cross, and they are marked by
subtle reflections, true theologies that seek to

understand the life of Jesus, his violent death, and his resurrection.

Each of the Gospels represents a particular community that, during the so-called dark years (between his death and the writing of the Gospel texts), produced reflections on the human and divine meaning of Jesus. They combine historical memory, theology, and the missionary intention to expand the new way of speaking of God (the Trinity), to announce the good news of the kingdom, and to witness to the event of the resurrection as the great hope of humanity.

This combination of recollections of historical facts and theological reflections, and even the direct production of theology, represents the effort of those first communities to understand and announce what Jesus lived and demonstrated: the lovingkindness of God-Abba for all. Thus, for example, the accounts of the infancy of Jesus seem to be a theological production. However, this set of factors does not make it clear, in strictly historical terms, which was the *ipsissima vox Jesu* (his original voice) and which was the *ipsissima intentio Jesu* (his fundamental project).

3

Jesus's Fundamental Project: Uniting Our Father with Our Bread

A ssuming a whole exegetical investigation that cannot be summarized here, many scholars affirm that it is in the prayer of the Our Father (Lk 11:2-4; Mt 6:9-13) that we discover his fundamental project. Curiously, in this prayer of the Our Father, there is no information that is considered essential to the Christian faith, such as the mystery of the incarnation, the Church, the hierarchy, the Eucharist, the Trinity. What is important is *our* Father, his salvific plan which is the *Kingdom*, and

Our Bread, the human being in his basic needs. It is worth clarifying that Jesus calls God Abba, an expression without parallel in all Jewish literature, a childish language that no one would use to refer to God. But Abba reveals a relationship of intimacy and total trust such as one has, in everyday life, with one's father or grandfather. Jesus uses the expression Abba, Dear Daddy, 170 times.

When the disciples ask Jesus: "Lord, teach us to pray" (Lk 11:1), something that every Jew knows very well, what they are trying to do, by means of a linguistic detour, is to say to him: "Lord, make us clearly understand your fundamental intention or what the slogan of your message is." Jesus then reveals his original intention in the form of a prayer. It is the Lord's Prayer, now prayed throughout Christendom.

In summary, we can affirm that the essence of the message contained in this prayer resides in these two poles: *Our Father* and *Our Bread* within the scope of the kingdom, which is

God's ultimate and supreme project for humanity and all creation.

If we look closely, this revealing prayer,
which Tertullian, perhaps the most eminent
lay theologian of ancient Christianity, who
came from North Africa, called the "summary
of the whole gospel" (*breviarium totius evan-
gelii*), responds to three fundamental hungers
of every human being:

The existence of Someone who can welcome us
in a definitive way, just as we are; hence the
figure of God-Abba.

Another insatiable hunger is for an *ultimate
and full meaning* for all that exists in heaven
and on earth, always present in human life,
and from which emerges the figure of the
kingdom.

The third hunger, which can be satisfied
but without which the others would lose their
ground, is that of *bread*, the daily food that
guarantees the continuity of life on Earth.
Only those who always keep *Our Father* and

Our Bread united in the perspective of a final and full meaning, the kingdom, can say Amen.

In history we know polarizations: there are those who celebrate Our Father, sing and dance for his goodness, forgetting Our Bread. And there are those who, on the contrary, fight and sacrifice themselves for Our Bread, forgetting Our Father. Both represent liberations, but they are insufficient and do not respond to the three fundamental hungers of the human being. They are not in consonance with the tradition of Jesus.

Certainly, critical exegesis identifies other words of the historical Jesus as sure data; for example, the Beatitudes, certain miracles, and especially the cry from the top of the cross, maintained by the evangelists in its Hebrew/Aramaic formulation: *Eloi, Eloi, lema sabach-thani*: "My God, my God, why have you forsaken me?" (Mk 15:34).

Since we are in the realm of history, without devaluing its *objective* dimension (his divinity), we are interested in the *subjective* dimension, that is, the interior process of Jesus that led him to feel that he was the Son of God–Abba.

4

Strict Monotheism to Trinitarian Monotheism

This process is extremely surprising, in a certain sense shocking, because the entire Jewish tradition, from the earliest times to the present day, consists of affirming a strict monotheism before the world, the sovereignty of *one* true God. The Jews condemned to the gas chambers in the Nazi extermination, the *Shoah*, entered singing the *Shema Israel, Adonai Echad*: "Hear, O Israel, our God is one."

How is it possible that someone now dares to break this tradition of martyrs in the name

of the one true God and proclaim himself
to be the Son of God? Is it blasphemy? Is it
madness? It is neither blasphemy nor madness,
but the proclamation of another understanding of God, who is one and the same, but
who willed companions in his life, who fully
communicated himself to humanity through
the Son of the Father who became incarnate
in our flesh (Jn 1:14) and through the Spirit
who makes his dwelling in Mary of Nazareth
(Lk 1:35). It is necessary to understand what
this divine claim of Jesus represents for the
faithful Jews, even to do them justice. They
showed immense difficulty in accepting Jesus
as the Son of God and acting in his name.

Even among Christians we know how difficult and long the intellectual battle was to
profess that "Jesus Christ is true God and
true man, with the same essence as the Father
according to his deity, and the same essence
with us according to his humanity"—affirmed
at the Council of Chalcedon in 451. The way
to this profession of faith was paved by a long

process that conferred the same divine nature on the creative Spirit that impelled Jesus in his liberating preaching and gave cohesion to the first apostolic community on the Jewish feast of Pentecost. This culminated in the Christian creed at the Council of Constantinople (381), in which Christian faith, piety, and reflection definitively assumed the trinitarian nature of God as Father, Son, and Holy Spirit.

In this way the trinitarian way of conceiving and speaking of God as a God-communion, a God-love, a God-relation bursts forth. It is about the mutual indwelling (*perichoresis*) among the divine Persons, so essential that it allows us to speak of a single living God who eternally self-reveals as a God whose nature is relational. *In the beginning is not the solitude of the One, but the communion of the Three.* They are so intertwined and involved in one another, for one another, and with one another, that a single God-love, a single God-communion, a single essential God-relationship emerges. There arises a monotheism, which is no longer strict, but trinitarian. It is no longer the same conception, shared by Jews and Muslims, of a radical monotheism. Due to the relational nature of God, a trinitarian type of monotheism emerges.

5

The Importance
of Jesus's Baptism:
The Awareness of Being the
Son of God-Abba

Having made these necessary observations, we can now ask ourselves how Jesus's interior process of feeling that he was the beloved Son of God-Abba *took place*. We answer: this event took place on the occasion of Jesus's baptism by John the Baptist (Mk 1:9–11; Mt 3:13–17; Lk 3:21–22). There he heard an interior voice: "You are my beloved Son, with you I am well pleased," or, according to an early variant of the reliable code D, "I have begotten you."

The dominant Christologies hardly address this question of the subjectivity of Jesus. They run the risk of psychologizing the experience of Jesus. They cling to a strict historicity, even though they are aware of the impossibility of doing a biography of Jesus, as was demonstrated in the great work of Albert Schweitzer, before he became a doctor in Lambaréné, in Gabon, Africa. This conception was radicalized by Rudolf Bultmann, who in his famous book *Jesus and the Word*, the result of decades of studies on "form criticism" (*formgeschichte*) and "redaction criticism" (*Redactiongeschichte*), presents the most certain data on the historical Jesus without including the event of the resurrection. For him, the resurrection places us before a transhistorical event (not empirically apprehensible) that can only be grasped by faith.

For this reason, the resurrection escapes the eye of the investigator of the historicity of Jesus of Nazareth. If a camera had been installed in the tomb of Jesus, it would not have captured the resurrection, because it is situated at another level of reality, not empirically graspable by our ordinary senses or devices, because it occurs in the dimension of the divine, which by its nature is not empirically graspable. However, it is not nonexistent. It happened, it is an event, but on a transempirical level, only graspable by the organ of faith.

We do not fear the criticism of psychologization. That is not what this is about. It is about something that certainly involves the human psyche of Jesus, but it goes beyond that. It affects him more deeply at a level of the essence of being (ontological), which goes beyond merely psychic limits. Jesus had more than a *spiritual experience* which, as the words suggests, is restricted to the experiential and sensitive realm. The experience is deeper, because it embraces the whole of Jesus's existence. Therefore, its essential (ontological) character involves his whole being: the psyche, the deep consciousness, the original will, and the total openness to the Infinite. Such an event means an experience that goes beyond the mere experiential.

We will see later on the steps taken by the carpenter-craftsman who, starting from the darkness of his consciousness, grew to the full light of a clear consciousness of himself, which made him feel loved by the Father-Abba and, thus, the Son of his "Dearest Daddy."

This datum is original to Jesus, and it is up to theology to trace it, not out of curiosity, but for a devout reason that realizes that we are before a Mystery that reveals itself and that remains a Mystery. We must respect the way in which the awareness of being the beloved Son slowly took shape in the discourse, in the interiority of the man Jesus of Nazareth, until he had the founding experience of feeling himself to be the Son of the Father and began to preach and act as the Son who announces and realizes the project of that kind and loving Father: his kingdom.

I am convinced that this original and unique experience really happened. We know the circumstance: it was on the occasion of his baptism by John the Baptist. If we leave aside the accounts of Jesus's infancy given to us by the evangelists Matthew and Luke, which are considered to be late constructions full of theological significance, all the evangelists begin with the *baptism of Jesus by John the Baptist*.

When Jesus heard the fame of John the Baptist, who came out of the wilderness, where he subsisted on locusts and wild honey, baptizing by the Jordan River, a devout man, he joined the crowd and also went to see what was happening. Crowds of people came from all over Palestine, for the Baptist preached the imminent arrival of the kingdom (the new order willed by God) and demanded penance from the people in view of this coming irruption. Probably, as the evangelist John hints (3:22), Jesus would have stayed for some time with John the Baptist, since three of his disciples were attracted by Jesus and became his followers: Andrew, Simon. and Philip. But in spite of some convergences (need for conversion and expectation of the kingdom), Jesus differs from the Baptist: he has an original experience of God-Abba, he does not announce a God-judge, but a God-Abba, a Daddy, a Father of immense goodness.

In any case, Jesus joined the crowd and allowed himself to be baptized. It was precisely at this moment that Jesus came to the full and lucid awareness of being the beloved Son of the Father. A torrent of spiritual love invaded his whole being and radically transformed his life. We now find ourselves before the foundational root of all theological reflection, based on the interiority of Jesus, therefore on a Jesuology, on the historical Jesus who feels and lives as the Son of God the Father, kind and merciful.

6

The Original Experience

Let us go deeper into the nature of Jesus's experience at his baptism by John the Baptist. First of all, we realize that, in all religions except Christianity, human beings seek God. In the Jesus tradition, however, it is God who seeks human beings. In the others, God is sought through verbal prayer, silent meditation, observance of religious and ethical precepts, participation in feasts and rites, and the memory of traditions. The more upright and faithful a person is, the more worthily he or she approaches God.

In the Jesus tradition, the opposite is true: God seeks out human beings, especially those

who feel lost, are not guided by ethical prin-
ciples, and even believe that they have been
abandoned by God. Logically, in this tradition
we also pray and preserve religious traditions,
live ethically, and attend cults and feasts. In
short, one *observes the Law*. But this is not
where the novelty lies. Without invalidating
these religious facts, the uniqueness brought
by Jesus is captured another way, that of his
profound *spiritual experience* of the love of
God–Abba.

In an obscure village, Nazareth, so in-
significant that it never appears in the Old
Testament scriptures and somewhat despised
("Can anything good come out of Nazareth?"
(Jn 1:46), lives an unknown man whose name
never appeared in the profane or religious
chronicles of the time, neither in Jerusalem
nor in Rome. He belongs to the group of the
so-called poor of the land, the invisible ones.
But his chief characteristic consists in living
a deep faith in the God of the fathers, Abra-
ham, Isaac, and Jacob, with an unshakable

confidence that God will fulfill what the prophets announced: justice for the poor, protection of widows, and elevation of the humiliated and offended. That man is precisely Jesus of Nazareth.

As we have already mentioned, by profession he is a craftsman-carpenter and farmer, like his father, Joseph. Until adulthood he lived with his family the "spirituality of the poor of Yahweh." He was known in the village as "the son of Joseph, whose father and mother we know" (Jn 6:42) or simply "the carpenter, son of Mary" (Mt 13:55) or "the son of Joseph" (Lk 4:22).

But he showed a singularity that perplexed his own parents. He did not call God "Lord," as was customary, but instead in a very peculiar way: Abba, a childish diminutive of "Dear Daddy." This became clear when, at the age of twelve, he participated with his parents in the annual pilgrimage to Jerusalem and got lost in the Temple (see Lk 2:41–52). When his parents found him and asked, "Why have you treated us like this?" he said to them, "Did you not know that I must be in my Father's house?" His parents were perplexed; they did not understand this unheard-of language. But Mary, nontheless, kept it in her heart. And there it all remained. Nothing is known of his subsequent hidden family and professional life. Only the evangelist Luke later noted in his Gospel, written around the year 80 CE: "Jesus increased in wisdom and in years and in divine and human favor."

Exegetical commentaries have given little importance to the baptism of Jesus by John the Baptist. For us, however, it is the decisive event that changed the meaning of the life of the carpenter-craftsman of Nazareth.

The fact is that the moment came when, together with the multitude and not alone, as usually depicted in art, Jesus entered the water. At a sign from the Baptist, together with all those present, he was immersed in the waters of the Jordan River and was thus baptized.

But something very singular happened to him. After he was baptized, while he "was praying," says the text of Luke (3:21), he felt a tremendous interior tremor. He was overcome by a wave of love so overflowing that it moved his whole being: "You are my Son, the Beloved; with you I am well pleased" (Mk 1:10–11; Mt 3:17). Luke is more explicit and refers, in a version of the D code, possibly more original, to what Jesus heard within himself: "You are my beloved Son, *I have begotten you*" (Lk 3:21–22). The biblical language points to the inner experience using pictorial and symbolic expressions: "the heaven was opened. and the Holy Spirit descended upon him in bodily form like a dove. And a voice came from heaven." How can we adequately express a radical interior experience using pictorial and symbolic expressions? These metaphors used by the evangelists constitute a mise-en-scène to express something highly original and the radicality of a unique spiritual experience lived by Jesus. Words are incapable of expressing it; it is only symbols that can speak to the depths of the human being, as the psychoanalytic tradition teaches us.

From that moment on, the "conversion" of Jesus took place, a true revolution in his life. He felt that he was the beloved Son of the beloved God-Abba. He is invaded by a passion of divine love, by a paternal tenderness that took hold of his whole life. He experienced directly the lovingkindness of God, a presence so powerful that it affected his whole being, his whole consciousness, and his whole existence. He became another. Whoever calls God "Father," logically feels that he is his Son.

Let us observe that it is no longer Jesus who seeks God when he piously goes to the Jordan River where the Baptist baptized. It is God who seeks him and reveals him as his beloved Son. This is the great revolution operated by God-Abba in Jesus of Nazareth. From this unique experience he detaches himself from his family and gives himself body and soul to the proclamation of a great novelty: the love of God-Abba and the coming of the kingdom of God. He left Nazareth and went to live in Capernaum, north of Lake Gennesaret.

The Great Transformation: Feeling the Unconditional Love of God-Abba

As in all things, there is always a process. It was no different with Jesus of Nazareth. Little by little he became aware of God's loving closeness until full consciousness came to him when he was baptized in the River Jordan. According to some, he was then in his early thirties.

It is one thing to be *objectively* the beloved Son of God, which he can be from the moment of his conception. It is another thing for him to be *subjectively* aware of this, to know its times and movements in a slow and constant *crescendo* accompanying the various stages of his life. In the baptism in the Jordan River, this leap to full and clear consciousness took place precisely on the occasion of this experiential visitation of God-Abba.

Herein lies the great singularity recounted by the evangelists: to bear witness to the *lovingkindness of God,* the God who becomes closer than a neighbor, the God who seeks a radical intimacy with the human being, in this case with Jesus of Nazareth. This love is unconditional and universal. It includes all human beings, regardless of their moral condition and life situation, because we are all interdependent and united by the bonds of the same humanity. When God-Abba approaches Jesus so intimately, he approaches, in the same act, all his brothers and sisters who share with him the same humanity, the same life, with its lights and shadows. This is what the Council of Chalcedon (341) means when it affirms the full humanity of Jesus, equal to our own. It is the gratuitous overflow of the love of God-Abba in Jesus and toward his human sons and daughters, brothers and sisters of Jesus, as never before in history. From now on, *God*-Abba is in our midst. To put it in scholarly theological language: God-Abba has communicated himself fully and unreservedly to Jesus of Nazareth. Through his beloved Son, he is in our midst. Jesus is God present in our fragile and mortal flesh. Not without reason, St. Matthew the Evangelist will later record that his name is *Emmanuel* (Mt 1:23), which means "God with us."

With this, a new path is inaugurated, different from that of the observance of the Law and the distinctions made between good and bad, just and unjust. These things, we acknowledge, have their reason for being in human coexistence. But this is not how God sees and judges human beings.

Jesus's look and logic are of a totally different nature. In him, an unconditional divine love bursts forth, beginning with one of those who never usually speak, who have never attended a school of theology, or at the most, the small biblical school next to the synagogue. The Nazarene comes from this milieu. He does not belong to the world of scholars, jurists, the priestly caste, or a certain social status. He is an anonymous man, more accustomed to manual labor than to the use of words.

Suddenly, everything changed; flooded by the loving closeness of God, he began to preach with such enthusiasm and wisdom that his listeners commented: "Where did this man get all this? What is this wisdom that has been given to him? What deeds of power are being done by his hands? Is not this the carpenter, the son of Mary?" (Mk 6:2-3; Mt 13:54-55). His family was so perplexed that "they went out to restrain him, for people were saying, "He has gone mad" (Mk 3:21). Yes, he is mad, a prisoner of the divine madness of God's unconditional love and of his loving closeness to all human beings, beyond any social or moral condition.

8

How Jesus Reveals God-Abba's Love to People of Ill Repute

Jesus's privileged ones are the poor, always despised; he eats with sinners; he approaches the tax collectors, hated by the people for being allies of the Roman occupying forces (Mk 2:16). He is even called a glutton and a drunkard (Mt 11:19), because he accepts the invitation to eat in the house of sinners (Lk 15:2; Mt 9:10–11). He broke the religious taboos of the time by conversing with a Samaritan woman, considered a heretic (Jn 4:7–15), by defending another woman caught in adultery, and by allowing a sinner to kiss his feet and anoint them with an expensive perfume, drying them with her hair, amid copious tears. A great scandal arose because she was considered of ill repute (Lk 7:37–39). None of this mattered to Jesus. She was worthy to experience the love of God-Abba. Why does Jesus take on such attitudes that are considered scandalous? Because he wants to bring to everyone, especially the socially disqualified, the lepers, the paralyzed, the blind, but also the public sinners, the scribes, the fervent Pharisees, the women, even the collaborators of the Romans, to tax collectors, to desperate people crying out for healing, to heretics (Samaritans), and to foreigners (like the Syrophoenician woman and a Roman official), the news that God has approached them all with unconditional love.

Jesus, completely taken by this love of God-Abba, turns to his brothers and sisters and shows them with his attitudes this newness of God's loving and unconditional closeness. He also becomes for everyone the *Dearest Daddy*. What is decisive is not the Law and the carefully observed traditions, but rather to accept what God-Abba said to Jesus and now repeats to them, no matter what they do in life. He simply says to them: "You are my sons and daughters, my beloved ones; with you I am well pleased" (cf. Mk 1:11). This sounds first of all astonishing, and then comes an unheard-of joy and a feeling of liberation.

Jesus's first word is: "The time is fulfilled, and the kingdom of God has come near; repent, and believe in the good news" (Mk 1:15). The crowd is ecstatic and many follow Jesus.

But this is only one side of the reality. It implies another side, that is, that this amazing proposal needed and still needs an answer. It requires a change of mindset and a change of heart. That is what *metanoia* means. And what happened? This is the decisive question. A proposal requires a responsible response. And unfortunately this did not happen.

The kingdom, contrary to Jewish expectations, was not the restoration of the old order, the political liberation from Roman domination of which they were so ashamed. For Jesus, the kingdom of God is something else. It consists of a new relationship of love among people—men and women, including those of ill repute; foreigners; and heretics—including everyone, even the ungrateful and the wicked (Lk 6:35). What prevails now is that lovingkindness, made of welcome and boundless mercy.

9

There Is No Eternal Condemnation, Only Temporary

I f this love is so radical, there can be no exclusion of anyone, no condemnation forever. Condemnation is a creation of society. It decides who is inside and who is outside the juridical status it has defined communally. For God-Abba there is no outside. All are included, because all are sons and daughters, before any other determination.

Very much in the spirit of the historical Jesus, the Evangelist John has Jesus say: "Anyone who comes to me I will never drive away" (Jn 6:37). God knows no eternal condemnation, because his mercy is boundless. If there were eternal condemnation, God would have "lost." And God can never lose!

> For you love all things that exist
> and detest none of the things that
>   you have made,
> for you would not have formed
>   anything if you had hated
>   it. . . .
> You spare all things, for they are
>   yours, O Lord, you who love
>   the living. (Wis 11:24-26)

He leaves the ninety-nine sheep sheltered in the sheepfold and goes in search of the stray one until he finds it.

Pope Francis, addressing the new African cardinals, said: "Do not do what has been done historically, an evangelization of fear and terror of hell. Jesus, true God and true man, conquered death, rose from the dead and wants to be reborn in the hearts of all: no one, however wounded by evil, is condemned on this earth to remain separated from God forever." In *Misericordiae vultus*, he says peremptorily: "Mercy will always be greater than any sin, and no one can place limits on the love of God who is ever ready to forgive (no. 3)."

Psalm 103, one of the most hopeful biblical texts, attests to this. Speaking of God it says:

> He will not always accuse, . . .
> As a father has compassion for his
>   children,
>   so the Lord has compassion for
>   those who fear him.
> For he knows how we were made;
>   he remembers that we are
>   dust. . . .
> But the steadfast love of the Lord is
>   from everlasting to everlasting.
>   (Ps 103: 6-17)

This innovative message of Jesus—the unconditional love and boundless mercy of

God-Abba—was and is so revolutionary that it has not taken root to the point of being lived by all. It is still not taken up by the majority of human beings, not even by the baptized. This was the case in Jesus's time, when he wandered the rocky roads of Palestine. It should not be forgotten that it was mainly the religious, aligned with the politicians, who condemned him and led him to the cross. And even today this message of the historical Jesus remains an appeal to all.

The great tragedy experienced by Jesus was the fact that this love of the merciful God-Abba was not accepted: "He came to what was his own, and his own people did not accept him" (Jn 1:11). That is why they crucified him, because there was no acceptance. This rejection continues through the centuries to the present day, perhaps even more fiercely, as hatred and discrimination sweep the vast, now unified world. It is likely to be so, unfortunately, until the end of time.

No matter. Although he felt himself to be the Son of God-Abba, he

> did not regard equality with God
> as something to be grasped,
> but emptied himself,
> taking the form of a slave,
> assuming human likeness.
> And being found in appearance as a
>   human,
> he humbled himself
> and became obedient to the point
>   of death—
> even death on a cross. (Phil 2:6-8)

10

The Great Rejection of God-Abba's Unconditional Love

B ecause of the love that burned within him, Jesus took upon himself, alone, this kind of accursed death, the cross and all the pains of the world. He accepted all kinds of slander against him; the betrayal of two apostles, Judas and Peter; the fate of those who over the centuries no longer believe or feel abandoned by God. He bore the doubts and tribulations of them all. He even received death threats that later became reality.

Like so many in the world, he too "went through the same trials as we do; he addressed prayers and supplications between cries and tears to the one who could save him from death and was not heeded [in a more original and ancient version, different from the current one, of Code D], despite being his Son." "Although he was a Son, he learned obedience through what he suffered," says an anonymous disciple of St. Paul, author of the epistle to the Hebrews (Heb 5:7-8). Moreover, he was seized by anguish and fear to the point that "his sweat became like great drops of blood falling down on the ground" (Lk 22:44) in Gethsemane, on the Mount of Olives, when he was about to be arrested, tortured, and condemned.

On the cross, almost on the verge of despair, in communion with all those who also feel the absence of God, he cried out: "My God, why have you forsaken me" (Mk 15:34). The love of God was in Jesus, but it was withdrawn so that he could participate in the human hell of the "death of God" suffered by many people. All these will never be alone.

The Christian creed says that he "descended into hell," that is, he experienced absolute solitude, with no one to accompany him. But God-Abba was also there, because absence is also a form of presence. From that moment on, no one will be alone in the hell of extreme human loneliness. Jesus, with his love and solidarity, was and will be with all of them forever.

The resurrection of Jesus represents a true *insurrection* against the religion of the Law and the justice of the time. It appears as a flash that will reveal, in fullness, the love of God, which has never failed. It was fully there, in Jesus suffering with those who suffer, and now rising with all those who will rise, participating in his resurrection (Rom 8:29). According to biblical interpretation, the resurrection of the Messiah is never only personal. It includes his entire human and cosmic community.

If so, it means that the resurrection is still in process. Jesus has not just risen. He is on his way to Galilee, as St. Mark the Evangelist says, to show himself there (16:7). He will find the fullness of his resurrection when all of humanity and the cosmos also reach their fullness, that is, when they are transfigured and resurrected, when they fully realize all the potentialities that they carry within them. Deniers and atheists are free to be what they are, not to accept or even know this love of God. But this changes nothing for the God-Abba, who never abandons them, because they never cease to be his sons and daughters. For them he repeats: "You are my beloved sons and daughters, in you I find my joy."

But it is worth reflecting on this: If we cannot see a star in the sky, it is not the star's fault, but the limitation of our eyes. Boundless love and boundless mercy reach all of us too. We are embraced by God-Abba, even if we refuse to embrace him. Though unseen, the star will continue to shine. You can even say, as some people believe Jean-Paul Sartre said on his deathbed: "I remain an atheist, but I nevertheless have the hope that God exists, otherwise life would have no meaning."

True and real Christianity consists in living this experience initiated by Jesus, who founded his tradition and his way. Most Christian churches are organized around a *sacred power* that creates inequalities, hierarchies, and divisions between clergy and laity. In the Roman Catholic Church this is clearly expressed in a thick doctrinal book called the *Catechism of the Catholic Church*. One feels like a hostage who is bound to a certain dogmatic and moral order, to a pious life, to the reception of the sacraments, to the participation in the liturgical feasts. All this is not unimportant, certainly, but it is not yet the following of Jesus or the experience and living of the newness that he brought to humanity. We can be pious Catholics, but that does not yet mean that we are true Christians who feel penetrated by the love and mercy of God in the following of Jesus.

For the other Christian churches, and also for other religions, the challenge launched by Jesus of Nazareth continues, now transformed into the religious and ethical heritage of humanity: to live unconditional love and try to love in the way of God and in the way of Jesus, privileging those whom he privileged, the last ones, those who do not count.

Where power reigns, no matter whether secular or religious, love does not flourish, tenderness does not flourish, and the love of God-Abba and his boundless mercy is obscured.

It cannot be denied that, historically, a part of the Roman Catholic Church was and still is closer to the palaces than to the grotto of Bethlehem, that it proclaims Christ king of the universe and forgets that he is a king with a crown of thorns and a mantle of scorn.

11

The Reversal:
The Conversion of the
Prodigal Son's Father

How different everything would be in this world if this unprecedented revolution had flourished among us. There would not be what we are now witnessing in this new phase of humanity, living in the same common home, that is, the predominance of hatred, discrimination, violence against those who cannot defend themselves, against women, against LGBTQ persons, or any other minorities, and especially today against nature, the very base that sustains our life.

This is why Jesus, although he is risen, continues to allow himself to be crucified with all the crucified of history in all their most diverse forms. His resurrection is not yet complete, for his brothers and sisters, and the whole universe of which they are a part, have not yet attained the fully realized resurrection.

The Parable of the Prodigal Son reveals what the tradition of Jesus is like. What is new and surprising is not the *conversion of the son,* who returns, repentant, to his father's house. It is *the conversion of the father,* who, full of mercy and kindness, embraces, kisses, and organizes a party for the son who squanders his inheritance. The only one criticized is the "good son," a follower of the Law. Everything about him was perfect. But for Jesus, it is not enough to be good, to follow the Law perfectly. He lacked the main thing, that is, the feeling of mercy and love of God-Abba, toward his brother, who was lost in the world.

12

Jesus and the Temptations in the Wilderness

Whenever one feels overwhelmed by an overpowering experience, one feels the need to withdraw, to meditate, to deepen the experience, and to realize its full meaning. So it was with Jesus and, later, with Paul of Tarsus. Paul had the experience of the Risen One (Acts 9:3–6), underwent a profound transformation, and withdrew to Arabia to contemplate the experience. Only then did he return to Damascus. Three years later he went to Jerusalem to meet with the fathers of the faith (Gal 1:16–18).

Something similar happened to Jesus. Shortly after the intimate and extraordinary experience of love and of feeling himself the beloved Son of God-Abba, he went into the desert and stayed there for forty days and forty nights (Mk 1:12–13; Mt 4:1–11; Lk 4:1–13).

In the wilderness, Jesus is confronted with three types of power: *prophetic, political,* and *religious.* The Synoptic Gospels call this story "the temptations of Jesus" plotted by the devil.

Biblical hermeneutics understands that the temptations of Jesus occurred within him. In his mind appears the figure of the "tempter," as St. Matthew the Evangelist describes him (4:3). We must not conceptualize this "tempter" as an external being. Just as the experience of divine love took place in the deepest interiority of Jesus, expressed metaphorically in the form of a dove, the open sky, and a voice, so it was with the temptations. The temptations circulated in the mind of Jesus, real temptations, cited by the "tempter," Satan, before which Jesus had to take sides.

Jesus rejects the three forms of power, for he understands his mission in the light of Isaiah's Suffering Servant:

> he has borne our infirmities
> and carried our diseases, . . .
> and the Lord has laid on him
> the iniquity of us all. . . .
> Out of his anguish he shall see;
> he shall find satisfaction through
> his knowledge.
> The righteous one, my servant,
> shall make many righteous,
> and he shall bear their iniquities.
> (Is 53:4, 6, 11)

Therefore, the path of the beloved Son of God-Abba will not be the pomp and glory with which every power is clothed, but the path of the renunciation of all power and of a humility transformed into humiliation, assumed in solidarity with all the humiliated and offended of history.

As many exegetes maintain, it is very likely that Jesus discovered his true vocation in the light of the texts of Isaiah (chapters 52 and 53), in which the redemptive destiny of the Suffering Servant is described.

Returning to temptations, we know that power represents an extremely powerful archetype, present in all human beings. Thomas Hobbes testifies to this in Chapter XI of his famous *Leviathan*:

> I put for a general inclination of all mankind a perpetual and restless desire of power after power, that ceaseth only in death. And the cause of this is not always that a man hopes for a more intensive delight than he has already attained to, or that he cannot be content with a moderate power, but because he cannot assure the power and means to live well, which he hath present, without the acquisition of more.

Power gives the human being the feeling of being a little god who can decide about his life and the lives of others. It can take the form of a tyrannical power, a shared power, or a power of service. If left unchecked, power, by its internal logic, always wants more power; it associates with other powers to be stronger, because power does not allow itself to be weak lest it be absorbed by a stronger power. The use of power is a great challenge and a real temptation for the human being. Is it a power to dominate? Is it a power to reinforce the power of others? Is it a power at the service of the common good? Only those who know how to exercise power well keep their distance from it, and avoid all conceit and arrogance.

The first temptation is that of *prophetic power*: to turn stones into bread (Mt 4:1–4). Bread guarantees life and survival. A bearer of power can, by giving it as alms, keep the hungry masses of humanity submissive. Political populism employs this strategy; instead of creating the conditions for the hungry to seek a means of earning their bread by means of work, it prefers to keep them hungry in order to make them dependent and thus dominate them by means of the alms of daily bread. Jesus rejects this form of power, quoting a text from Deuteronomy (8:3):

> "One does not live by bread alone,
> but by every word that comes from
> the mouth of God." (Mt 4:4)

The second temptation is that of *political power*, perhaps the most seductive. It is the power exercised by kings, dictators, presidents, potentates, owners of lands and fortunes who occupy high positions of power and use it to keep others dependent and even dominated. The temptation of Jesus is well characterized metaphorically by "a very high mountain" from which the tempter "showed him all the kingdoms of the world and their glory" (Mt 4:8). Everything can be Jesus's, provided that he yields to the tempter. "All these I will give you, if you will fall down and worship me" (Mt

4:9). In other words, power arrogates to itself an absolute character, possible only for God.

This is the original temptation, already described in the first pages of the Bible: "You will be like God" (Gen 3:5). Jesus again rejects this kind of power domination, quoting from Deuteronomy:

> "Away with you, Satan! for it is
>   written, 'Worship the Lord
>   your God,
> and serve only him.'" (Mt 4:10)

Jesus's path to follow is not that of pomp and glory, dominating all territories and persons, but that of presenting to them the love of God-Abba, accepted in freedom. His way is one of humility and service to every human creature, especially to the most helpless, his least brothers and sisters (Mt 25:40).

Finally, he is tempted by another type of power, also fascinating, *religious power*. This is very important and effective. Religion works with the ultimate meaning, worships God, and underlies ethical values. Despite the process of secularization, it must be recognized that most of humanity is governed by religious precepts. What ultimately counts more than ideology and economic interests are the convictions of faith, traditions, family, and the identity of a people. It is for these things that people strive and fight, and are even willing to give their lives, as is evident in the various forms of politico-religious fundamentalism.

Religious power is built on these fundamental facts. It influences the multitudes through its sacred values, ethics, traditions, rites, and celebrations. It is one of the most important factors in the identity of a people. Sacred power can introduce reforms both within the religion itself and within society. Religious power is often associated with political power, legitimizing it, as well as with popular power, validating the claims of the poor and oppressed who cry out for life and justice. In any case, religious power is always coveted by other powers due to its legitimizing character.

Jesus is tempted by this power as he is led to the Temple's pinnacle. The tempter plays his last card and challenges Jesus, as the Son of God, to perform a miracle, saying:

> "If you are the Son of God, throw yourself down, for it is written,
> 'He will command his angels concerning you,'
> and 'On their hands they will bear you up,
> so that you will not dash your foot against a stone.'" (Mt 4:6)

Jesus decisively rejects this temptation by quoting a text from Deuteronomy (6:16): "Do not put the Lord your God to the test" (Mt 4:7). Clearly Jesus does not imagine himself as a high priest who presides over a religion and religiously and ethically directs an entire people. He does not want to present a reform of the religion of the Law and the Torah. He does not advocate a political revolution to restore the throne of David. Nor does he miraculously turn stones into bread to satiate the hungry. His vocation is different, that of bearing witness to the unconditional divine Love that manifests itself in both the religious and profane spheres, through the Suffering Servant who gives himself to the others.

It should be emphasized that Jesus did not come to create a new religion; there were many already in the Roman Empire, and all were tolerated and present in the Pantheon of Rome. He came to *teach us to live* the values of the kingdom, which are unconditional love, solidarity without borders, compassion, and the ability to forgive without preconditions. He desired the new man and the new woman. This is the great nonviolent political-religious revolution that Jesus intended.

The Synoptic Gospels place the temptations at the beginning, even before Jesus begins his mission. They want to make it clear that his message is also one of power, not to be confused with the powers established and expected by the people, but of another nature, the power of unlimited and universal love.

Interestingly, having overcome these three temptations, Jesus undertakes a changes of place. At the invitation of the Baptist's former disciples Simon and Andrew, he leaves Nazareth, a small mountainside village of between two hundred and four hundred inhabitants, where he lived 90 percent of his life, and goes to live in Capernaum, a fishing village of about a thousand inhabitants, on the shores of Lake Gennesaret. From there he travels to neighboring towns such as Bethsaida, Chorazin, and Magdala, announcing his message.

13

The Spirituality of the Historical Jesus: His Three Passions

Whoever feels that he is a beloved Son, after having experienced the infinite love of God-Abba, bears witness to a profound spirituality.

By spirituality we mean the concrete experience of being a beloved Son. The experience occurs when we pass from the mind to the heart, the seat of a cordial or sensitive reason. It is the heart that feels, not the mind. For Jesus, the Son is not a concept of the mind, but an experience of the heart, both spiritual and emotional, so profound that it takes hold of his whole being. It is not a matter of thinking of himself as the Son of God-Abba, but of feeling and then thinking of himself fully from the heart. This is an absolutely original experience that left the Jews, who professed a strict monotheism, perplexed. Jesus goes beyond this monotheism and reveals to us an unconditional God-love, an unlimited God-communion that is made concrete historically in him, the beloved Son.

One of the reasons for his condemnation to death lies precisely in the fact that he acts in the name of God-Abba and implies that he is his Son. The high priest Caiaphas, says to him: "I put you under oath before the living God, tell us if you are the Messiah, the Son of God." Jesus simply replies, "You have said so." Caiaphas "tore his clothes and said, 'He has blasphemed!'" All present shouted, "He deserves death" (Mt 26:63–66).

The Gospel of John is even more explicit in putting into the mouths of those who wanted to stone him these words: "It is not for a good work that we are going to stone you but for blasphemy, because you, though only a human, *are making yourself God*" (Jn 10:33, emphasis added). In fact, he was not stoned but was condemned to the worst punishment, death on the cross, outside the city walls.

Three passions structure the spiritual experience of Jesus. The first, so deeply explored by St. John the Evangelist, is that of really feeling himself to be *the Son of God* and acting as God-Abba. The intimacy is so profound that he was able to say: "Whoever has seen me has seen the Father. . . . Do you not believe that I am in the Father and the Father is in me?" (Jn 14:9- 11). As he said previously, "The Father and I are one" (Jn 10:30). The Gospels note that he often withdrew to himself and spent the night in prayer (see, for example, Mt 14:23). We can imagine the deep communion with his beloved Abba and the paternal and filial dialogue that was then established. From this intimacy arose the strength to face the power of the anti-kingdom, the defamations, the slander, the threats of death, and even the torment of the cross. Since Jesus is the bearer of the same humanity as we are, his experience as a beloved Son opened a door so that all human beings can hear the same thing that Jesus did in his life. God-Abba said about Jesus on the occasion of his baptism: "You are my Son, the Beloved; with you I am well pleased" (Lk 3:22; Mk 1:11).

How different the history of humanity would be if this supreme dignity of being a son and daughter of God were to enter into the collective consciousness and permeate human relationships. Mahatma Gandhi had this very personal experience. When he saw someone violently beating an outcaste, he would intervene and say, "You cannot do this to a child of God." Being a son or daughter of God ultimately underlies the sacredness of every human being and his or her inviolable rights.

The second passion, with a political and holistic connotation, is that of the *kingdom of God.* Jesus does not proclaim himself, or the church, or the great traditions of the past. He announces the kingdom of God, a kingdom that has already come near and is in our midst (Mk 1:14; Lk 17:21).

Kingdom means the project of God-Abba that acts in the universe, in society, in the community, in personal life, healing the sick, liberating the oppressed, ending the empire of evil, and fully realizing all the latent potentialities both in the cosmos and in human beings. The kingdom represents an absolute revolution, utopia finally achieved, of the new man and the new woman, of the new heaven and the new earth.

This promise and this hope constituted the content of Jesus's preaching in every corner of Palestine. It was good news. That is why it aroused so much joy and enthusiasm in the crowds that listened to him. The first thing the apostles, especially St. Paul, announced when they entered the synagogues was the kingdom of God. Only afterward did they speak of the risen Jesus.

However, the kingdom was confronted with the anti-kingdom, that is, the presence of human evil, such as hatred, contempt, and death caused by the genocide of entire peoples throughout history. For this reason Jesus, in announcing the coming of the kingdom, calls for conversion, the renunciation of the kingdom of evil. To convert means to change one's mind and heart.

In his earthly saga, one has the impression that the anti-kingdom triumphed over the kingdom of God, because Jesus was finally crucified outside the city. But then came the resurrection, as the victory of the kingdom over the anti-kingdom, of full life over unjustly imposed death. For this reason, the ancient fathers of the church already interpreted the resurrection as the realization of the kingdom of God in the person of Jesus. The Risen One

is the *autobasileia tou Christou,* the self-realiza-
tion of the kingdom in the person of the risen
Jesus, in the words of Origen of Alexandria,
one of the greatest theologians of Christian
history. Now the good end of creation has
been anticipated. God's plan for his creation
has triumphed definitively: the kingdom has
arrived in all its fullness.

More important than the church is the
kingdom of God, which is realized in all times
and places. The church is its sacrament, that
is, its sign and instrument. Nothing more than
that. The kingdom overflows it, because it is in
the process of realization within history, not
parallel to it or in a part of it, as it would be
in the churches or only in those who profess
the Christian faith.

Where love is lived, justice is done, solidarity
is made concrete, compassion is nurtured, and
care for others and for all creation is inspired.
There, the goods of the kingdom are made
present; there the kingdom of God is realized
historically and procedurally, until it reaches

its fullness when the complete transfiguration of all things takes place, already symbolized in the risen body of Jesus. To live in the following of Jesus means to feel oneself an agent of the kingdom in the face of the anti-kingdom, until its complete establishment.

This is the original source of all Christian spirituality in the style of Jesus. It takes shape through the movements of the followers of Jesus and the Christian churches. It is also found in all those who live the values of the kingdom, such as love, compassion, and solidarity. They are the channels and not the crystal clear water of the source. The channel should not be identified with the source. This is why it is always important to distinguish, without separating, on the one hand, religion, the churches and Christian movements, and the people who live the goods of the kingdom, and on the other hand, spirituality. The latter is more fundamental, prior to its channeling, since it appears as the source that nourishes the various historical expressions of the heritage of Jesus. The latter comes later; spirituality is at its center.

The third passion that characterizes the spirituality of Jesus is his *love for the poor and the invisible*. He proclaims:

> "Blessed are you poor,
> for yours is the kingdom of God"
>   (Lk 6:20).

They are the first, not because they are good and more virtuous, but because, being poor, they are deprived of life in its fullness. And God-Abba is a living God, who, by his nature, is attracted to the oppressed and those condemned to lose their lives before their time.

Thus, all the Gospels attest—and this constitutes a firm historical core—to Jesus's compassion for the suffering, the sick, the blind, and all those rejected by society, such as the pagans and the Samaritan heretics. He never attacked women in the macho cultural context of the time, but always defended them, even if they were heretics, adulteresses, or women of ill repute. Because of this predilection, he was insulted and even threatened with death, to the point of having to hide in a city of refuge like Ephraim, near the desert, where he lived for a time with his disciples (Jn 11:54). A refugee in this city could not be arrested or handed over to the judicial authorities. Therefore, Jesus was not naive in facing death. He loved his life, and of course that of the apostles, and sought to safeguard them.

The kingdom begins with the last, as is clearly shown when he announces his liberating plan in the synagogue of Nazareth:

> "The Spirit of the Lord is upon me,
>   because he has anointed me
>   to bring good news to the poor.
> He has sent me to proclaim release
>   to the captives
>   and recovery of sight to the blind,
>   to set free those who are oppressed,

to proclaim the year of the Lord's
favor." (Lk 4:18–19)

Love extends unconditionally to all, but it has a special affinity for the marginalized and the invisible. To love one's neighbor as oneself, for Jesus, does not mean to love those who love us, but to love those whom no one loves or sees, even the ungrateful and wicked (Lk 6:32).

This spirituality, full of tenderness and passion, is at the spiritual foundation of the tradition of Jesus, at the foundation of the churches that perpetuate his memory and his following, so well reflected in all the writings that make up the New Testament, especially in the letters of St. Paul.

14

The Future of God's Radical
God-Abba and Jesus

We have experienced everything in the already long history of humanity, but we have not yet experienced, *collectively*, the kind of love in the style of Jesus and God-Abba. There has always been love between two or more people, but we have never tried to build a society whose *centrality* is unconditional love that includes everyone, even those usually unknown and invisible. What prevails in general terms is an insensitive and sometimes cruel and merciless society, which makes it difficult to love and care for one another, including loving and caring for nature.

However, many men and women have understood and lived the lovingkindness of God-Abba in the style of Jesus. These are the true bearers of Jesus's legacy, the witnesses of God's loving closeness, especially those mentioned in the Gospel of St. Matthew:

> "I was hungry and you gave me food, I was thirsty and you gave me something to drink, I was a stranger and you welcomed me, I was naked and you gave me clothing, I was sick and you took care of me, I was in prison and you visited me." (Mt 25:35–36)

To all of these he says: "Truly I tell you, just as you did it to one of the least of these brothers and sisters of mine, you did it to me" (Mt 25:40). In this is revealed the original experience of Jesus, who felt so united to God-Abba that he considered himself one with the Father (Jn 10:30; 14:9).

Will we ever succeed in making God's loving closeness a reality, regardless of people's moral, political, and ideological situations? Will this true world-transforming revolution take center stage? This is the great challenge of all evangelization: to bring to the whole world and to all people the awareness that they are loved by God-Abba and that they must live this love with everyone, that is, to bring them this good news.

The kingdom of God-Abba cannot be reached by any means whatsoever. Certainly those who have been criminals, violators of human sacredness, those considered sinners will need to pass through God's "clinic" to be cured of hatred and learn to love and adore God-Abba, who wants them close to him. They will first go through a process of purification, learning to love in order to live in heaven with those they have harmed, tortured, and murdered. For even they are not outside the rainbow of unconditional love, mercy, and the blessed grace of God-Abba and his beloved Son, Jesus.

15

The Emergence of a Christology Open to the Future

The divine Love experienced and witnessed by Jesus and ratified by the resurrection caused a tremendous spiritual shock to the apostles and their followers. They began to reason and to try to understand, in the light of the scriptures of the Old Testament, the saga of Jesus, the reason for his death, and, above all, the amazing event of the resurrection. Soon they began to celebrate his presence as the Risen One in hymns, in liturgies, and in rites, and to remember his life, his liberating deeds, and his central message, summarized in the prayer of the Our Father. Then they began to elaborate the doctrinal and central nuclei of his message, and thus arose the writings, the four Gospels. Behind them are communities that not only prayed but also reflected on the history and destiny of Jesus. They designed "the Way" of Jesus (Acts 19:9; 24:14). They set out to follow Jesus and to keep as their inheritance the memory of his sacred, unconditional, and universal saving love. They were indelibly touched by his profound humanity.

The early community, in its effort to understand what had happened to Jesus, began to bestow upon him titles of honor and excellence, such as teacher, prophet, the righteous, the good, the holy, and even the most sublime titles, such as Son of Man, Son of God, and, finally, God himself. *Christ* is used five hundred times, *Lord* three hundred and fifty times, *Son of Man* eighty times, *Son of God* seventy-five times, *Son of David* twenty times, and *God* three times.

Within thirty to forty years of his crucifixion and resurrection, Jesus attracted to himself the most noble, human and divine titles that existed in the Roman Empire. Each cultural group—Palestinian Jews, Judeo-Christians in the diaspora, and Hellenistic Christians—contributed to the process of deciphering who he ultimately was. Thus, for the *Palestinian community*, he emerges as the Messiah-Christ, the Son of Man, and the Son of God. For the *Jewish Christians in the diaspora*, Jesus is the new Adam, the Lord and the High Priest. The *Hellenistic Christian community* proclaims him as the Savior, the Head of the cosmos, the only begotten Son of the Father, and God himself.

In the end, it turns out that, not knowing how to define all the love of Jesus because of his intimate relationship with God-Abba, they ended up calling him by the supreme name of human language, beyond which one cannot go. They called him God: God incarnated in our misery and greatness. They thought: *A human being like Jesus can only be God himself.*

This process of deciphering did not end with calling Jesus God. God is a mystery that evokes other mysteries. The first is the mystery of the finite human being himself, capable of receiving the Infinite in himself, the mystery of the world, the mystery of the cosmos as a substratum without which there is neither human being nor Jesus, made Christ.

The very mystery of creation is linked to the mystery of Jesus Christ (see Jn 1:3; Eph 1:10; Col 1:15–18). Because it is a sacramental mystery, that is, visible and comprehensible but always a mystery for all understanding, it makes each generation of Jesus's followers return to the question that Jesus himself addressed to the apostles: "Who do you say that I am" (Lk 9:20; Mk 8:29; Mt 16:15). Christology arises as an answer to this question, as an effort of reverent and devout intelligence to deepen the understanding inherited from the past, through new contributions, new titles taken from the best that each culture has to offer. It should be clear that it is not the titles of excellence that constitute the greatness of Jesus. It is his love, the sovereignty he showed by acting in the name of God-Abba, that gave rise to all the titles, even the boldest and ultimate, that of God. By adding the name of Christ (the Anointed One, the Messiah) to the name of Jesus of Nazareth and by saying "Jesus Christ," we want to express the true humanity of Jesus (Jesuology) and, at the sam time, his true divinity (Christology).

The Council of Chalcedon (451) summed up well the common faith, the defining criterion that applies to this day to any community that refers to Jesus Christ to be considered church. It stated, as expressed in the *Catechism of the Catholic Church*:

> Following the holy Fathers, we unanimously teach and confess one and the same Son, our Lord Jesus Christ: the same perfect in divinity and perfect in humanity, the same truly God and truly man, composed of rational soul and body; consubstantial with the Father as to his divinity and consubstantial with us as to

his humanity; "like us in all things but sin."

It was the fascination aroused by Jesus of Nazareth, by his courageous and, at the same time, tender style, by his freedom from tradition, by the centrality he always gave to unconditional love, by his passion and death on the cross, but especially by his resurrection, that unleashed a torrent of reflections that were always incomplete and insufficient to say who Jesus was and who he is. In short, he is the ultimate expression of the love and close-ness of God-Abba, enfleshed in him as his beloved Son. As St. Paul will say in the Letter to the Colossians, around the years 58 and 60:

He is the image of the invisible God, the firstborn of all creature, for in him in heaven and on earth were created, things visible and invisible, whether thrones or dominions or rulers or powers—all things have been created through him and for him. . . . Christ is all and in all!" (Col 1:15–16; 3:11)

Dostoevsky offered a moving testimony about Jesus when he came out of the "House of the Dead," his time of harsh imprisonment in which he was subjected to hard labor:

Sometimes God sends me moments of peace. In those moments I love and feel that I am loved. It was in one of these moments that I composed my credo, where everything is clear and sacred for me. This creed is very simple. It goes like this: I believe there is nothing more beautiful, more profound, more empathetic, more human, and more perfect than Christ. And not only is there nothing, but I tell myself with a jealous love that there is not and cannot be. Moreover, if anyone could prove to me that Christ is outside the truth, and that the truth is not to be found in him, I would rather stay with Christ than with the truth.

The Love of Jesus and the Fate of Life on Earth

rancis of Assisi and Francis of Rome, together with a multitude of people, many of them anonymous, have dared to undertake this adventure, believing that by way of the loving care and loving closeness of God-Abba and Jesus there lies the liberation of human beings and the safeguarding of life and our imperiled Mother Earth.

The gravity of the present situation poses this dilemma: "No one is saved alone; we can only be saved together," as Pope Francis emphatically says in *Fratelli tutti* (no. 32). Mother

Earth is in constant labor pains until that day, which only God knows, when the new human, the new man and the new woman, is born. Together, along with nature itself, they will inhabit what Pope Francis calls "our common home"—the Magna Mater, Pachamama, the generous Mother Earth. Then, as prophesied by the German philosopher Ernst Bloch, author of the work *The Hope Principle*, "the true genesis is not at the beginning but at the end." Only thus do we comprehend that "God saw everything that he had made, and indeed, it was very good" (Gen 1:31).

Either we embody this dream of the Nazarene, who brought us the novelty of the love of God-Abba, the loving One who is always searching for us, even in the shadows of the valley of death, or we must fear for our destiny.

Instead of being the caretakers of creation, we have become the "Satan" of the earth that threatens all forms of life and especially human life with death. We inherited a paradise, and we are handing over to future generations a desert. But he who is in our midst as the Risen One, the cosmic Christ, will never abandon us or deny us his love and closeness. The God-Abba of the beloved Son has the power to forge from the ruins a new heaven and a new earth. Then all this will be past. The tears will be wiped away, the sad will be consoled, because they will be enfolded in the divine family of the Father, the Son, and the Holy Spirit. There will begin the true story of God-Abba with his beloved daughters and sons in his beloved only-begotten Son, and with the whole universe transfigured for all eternity.

Essential Bibliography

Barbaglio, Giuseppi. *Jesús, hebreo de Galilea.* Salamanca: Secretariado Trinitario, 2003.

Boff, Clodovis. *O cotidiano de Maria de Nazaré.* São Paulo: Editora Salesiana, 2009.

Boff, Leonardo. *Jesus Christ Liberator: A Critical Christology for Our Time.* Maryknoll, NY: Orbis Books, 2009.

———. *Passion of Christ, Passion of the World.* Maryknoll, NY: Orbis Books, 1987.

———. *The Question of Faith in the Resurrection of Jesus.* Chicago: Franciscan Herald Press, 1971.

———. *The Lord's Prayer: The Prayer of Integral Liberation.* Maryknoll, NY: Orbis Books, 1983.

———. *El Evangelio del Cristo Cósmico.* Madrid: Trotta, 2009.

————. *Way of the Cross, Way of Justice.* Maryknoll, NY: Orbis Books, 1980.

————. *O ovo da esperança: o sentido da festa da Páscoa.* Rio de Janeiro: Mar de Ideias, 2007.

————. O *Sol da esperança: Natal: histórias, poesias e símbolos.* Rio de Janeiro: Mar de Ideias, 2007.

————. *Christianity in a Nutshell.* Maryknoll, NY: Orbis Books, 2013.

————. *Holy Trinity, Perfect Community.* Maryknoll, NY: Orbis Books, 1990.

————, with Mark Hathaway. *The Tao of Liberation: Exploring the Ecology of Transformation.* Maryknoll, NY: Orbis Books, 2009.

————. *Thoughts and Dreams of an Old Theologian.* Maryknoll, NY: Orbis Books, 2022.

Castillo, José M. *Jesús: la humanización de Dios. Ensayo de cristología.* Madrid: Trotta, 2010.

Comblin, José. *Jesus of Nazareth.* Maryknoll, NY: Orbis Books, 1976.

Crossan, John Dominic. *Jesus: A Revolutionary Biography*. New York: HarperCollins, 1994.

———, with Jonathan L. Reed. *Excavating Jesus: Beneath the Stones, Behind the Texts*. New York: HarperCollins, 2003.

Ferraro, B. *Cristologia*. Petrópolis: Vozes, 2021.

Hoornaert, Eduardo. *Em busca de Jesus de Nazaré*. São Paulo: Paulus, 2016.

Leclerc, Eloi. *O reino escondido*. Petrópolis: Vozes, 1989.

Lohfink, Gerhard. *Jesus of Nazareth: What He Wanted, Who He Was*. Collegeville, MN: Liturgical Press, 2015.

Mesters, Carlos. *Com Jesus na contramão*. São Paulo: Paulus, 1995.

Moura Nunes, J. A., *Jesus de Nazaré: o melhor de nós*. Belo Horizonte: Ramalhete, 2019.

Onimus, J. *Jésus en direct*. Paris, Desclée de Brouwer, 1999.

Pagola, José Antonio. *Jesus: An Historical Approximation*. Miami, FL: Convivium Press, 2014.

————. *Volver a Jesús.* Madrid: PPC Editorial, 2014.

Schillebeeckx, Edward. *Jesus: An Experiment in Christology.* New York: Crossroad, 1981.

Sesboué, B. *Pedagogia de Cristo: elementos de cristologia fundamental.* São Paulo: Paulinas, 1997.

Sobrino, Jon. *Jesus the Liberator: A Historical-Theological Reading of Jesus of Nazareth.* Maryknoll, NY: Orbis Books, 1993.

————. *Christ the Liberator: A View from the Victims.* Maryknoll, NY: Orbis Books, 2001.

Theisen, Gerd. *El movimiento de Jesús: historia social de una revolución de los valores.* Salamanca: Ediciones Sígueme, 2005.